ROGER VERGÉ

The Main Course

Photography by SIMON WHEELER

THE MASTER CHEFS

TED SMART

ROGER VERGÉ has become synonymous with the food and sunshine of Provence, where he opened his Restaurant du Moulin de Mougins in 1969. His first book, *Ma Cuisine du Soleil* (1978), was translated into English as *Cuisine of the Sun*, and Cuisine du Soleil is the name of his cooking school in Mougins.

He is also the author of *Entertaining in the French Style* (1986) and *Roger Vergé's Vegetables in the French Style* (1994).

Roger Vergé was awarded the lifelong title Meilleur Ouvrier de France in 1972 and became a Chevalier de la Légion d'Honneur in 1987.

Photograph by J. C. Cliche

CONTENTS

Happy cooking consists of uniting natural products, seeking out simple harmonies, and enhancing each ingredient by the proximity of another complementary flavour.

INTRODUCTION

It was more than chance that brought me to Provence. Of course, its sunshine influenced my decision, but there is something here that is found nowhere else on earth: the air in Provence is full of the scents of herbs – rosemary, savory, sage, wild thyme, lavender and many others – and the flowers all smell of honey. Other aromas – olive oils, wines, sun-kissed fruits and vegetables – mingle in to delight the palate and excite the imagination of a chef.

I would even suggest that here, beside the Mediterranean, is the birthplace of French culture, not just gastronomic, but spiritual, architectural, artistic and sensual. Apart from butter and cream, which we replace with olive oil, all the wealth of French cuisine, the foundation of our culture, originates in the warmth of Provence.

Here, everything looks more real, more luminous, more intense and more full of joie de vivre. Is there any further need to explain why I live in Provence? In this book I have tried to capture some of the sunshine of Provence and share the happiness I find in its good food.

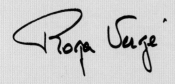

RED MULLET EN BARIGOULE

3 GLOBE ARTICHOKES
1 LEMON, HALVED
500 ML/16 FL OZ EXTRA VIRGIN
    OLIVE OIL
2 SMALL CARROTS, SLICED THINLY
2 SMALL ONIONS, SLICED THINLY
1 GARLIC CLOVE, CRUSHED
1 SPRIG OF THYME
2 BAY LEAVES
SALT AND PEPPER
150 ML/5 FL OZ DRY WHITE WINE
250 ML/8 FL OZ WHITE STOCK
2 LARGE RIPE TOMATOES, SKINNED
    (PAGE 28), SEEDED AND DICED
1 RED PEPPER, PEELED (PAGE 28)
    AND DICED
ABOUT 15 G/½ OZ EACH OF FRESH
    CHERVIL, DILL, TARRAGON, BASIL
4 SMALL RED MULLET, ABOUT
    200–225 G/7–8 OZ EACH,
    FILLETED

SERVES 4

Prepare the artichoke hearts (page 29) and leave them in the water.

Heat 200 ml/7 fl oz of the oil in a saucepan over low heat and sweat the carrots and onions until softened, about 5 minutes.

Add the garlic, thyme and bay leaves. Cut the artichoke hearts into quarters and add them to the pan with a little salt and pepper, the wine and stock. Simmer, uncovered, until the artichokes are tender and the sauce has almost evaporated, about 20 minutes.

Mix the diced tomatoes and pepper with most of the remaining olive oil; season to taste. Pick off the smallest, most tender herb leaves and chop them, but do not add them until the last moment.

Lightly brush the red mullet fillets with olive oil and place on a lightly oiled grill pan, skin side up. Place under a hot grill for 3–4 minutes, until just cooked.

Divide the artichokes between four plates and arrange the mullet on top. Mix the herbs with the tomato and pepper mixture and spoon over the fish.

MONKFISH CÔTE D'AZUR

675–800 G/1½–1¾ LB MONKFISH
   FILLETS
SALT AND PEPPER
1 SPRIG OF SAGE
8 BABY CARROTS
8 BABY TURNIPS
1 HEAD OF BROCCOLI, CUT INTO
   FLORETS
4 SMALL COURGETTES
12 SMALL NEW POTATOES
225 G/8 OZ MANGETOUT, SHELLED
   PEAS OR GREEN BEANS
1 BUNCH EACH OF SAGE AND
   ROSEMARY

THE SAUCE

1 TABLESPOON EACH OF CHOPPED
   FRESH PARSLEY AND CHERVIL
½ TABLESPOON EACH OF CHOPPED
   FRESH BASIL, TARRAGON, CHIVES
   AND CELERY LEAVES
1 GARLIC CLOVE
3 TABLESPOONS EXTRA VIRGIN
   OLIVE OIL
1 TABLESPOON WINE VINEGAR
1 TABLESPOON SMALL CAPERS
2 SMALL RIPE TOMATOES, SKINNED
   (PAGE 28), SEEDED AND DICED
½ RED PEPPER, PEELED (PAGE 28)
   AND DICED
3 TABLESPOONS PITTED BLACK
   OLIVES

SERVES 4

Remove the membrane from the monkfish. Place the fish on a piece of clingfilm, sprinkle with salt and pepper and add a leaf of sage every 1 cm/½ inch. Roll up very tightly to make a neat cylindrical shape. Place on a steamer rack and leave in a cool place.

Prepare all the vegetables, wash and arrange on a steamer rack; sprinkle with coarse salt.

Fill the bottom of a steamer with water, add the sage and rosemary and bring to the boil. Place the rack of vegetables over the water and steam for 10 minutes. Place the fish on its rack over the vegetables and steam for a further 10 minutes, or until both the fish and vegetables are tender.

Meanwhile, chop all the herbs for the sauce together with the garlic and mix with the oil, vinegar and salt and pepper to taste. Stir in the remaining ingredients.

Slice the monkfish and serve with the vegetables, with the sauce served separately.

STUFFED SEABASS

1 SEA BASS, ABOUT 900 G/2 LB,
   CLEANED, SCALED AND BONED,
   BONE RESERVED

SALT AND PEPPER

2 SMALL SHALLOTS, CHOPPED

50 ML/2 FL OZ DRY VERMOUTH

200 ML/7 FL OZ DRY WHITE WINE

100 G/3½ OZ BUTTER

100 ML/3½ FL OZ WATER

1 SMALL SPRIG OF THYME

1 SMALL BAY LEAF

150 ML/5 FL OZ DOUBLE CREAM

STUFFING

ABOUT 200 G/7 OZ WHITE FISH
   FILLET, WITH ITS BONE

1 OR 2 EGG WHITES

200 ML/7 FL OZ DOUBLE CREAM

125 G/4 OZ PEELED COOKED
   PRAWNS

2 TABLESPOONS PITTED SMALL
   BLACK OLIVES, CHOPPED

2 TABLESPOONS CHOPPED FRESH
   PARSLEY OR MIXED HERBS

SERVES 6

Preheat the oven to 160°C/325°F/
Gas Mark 3.

All the ingredients for the
stuffing must be cold. Place the
white fish fillet in a food processor
with a little salt and pepper and
purée briefly. Add the egg whites
and mix for a few seconds, then
add the cream and mix for a few
seconds more. Transfer to a bowl
and stir in the prawns, olives and
half the herbs.

Season inside the sea bass and
fill with the stuffing. Butter a
flameproof dish or baking tin and
sprinkle with salt, pepper and 1
chopped shallot. Place the sea bass
on top and pour in the vermouth
and half the wine. Bring to the
boil over medium-high heat, then
cover and bake for 40 minutes.

Sweat the remaining shallot in a
little butter with the fish bone for
2–3 minutes. Add the remaining
wine, bring to the boil, then add
the water, thyme, bay leaf and a
little pepper. Simmer very gently
for 10 minutes, then strain.

When the fish is cooked, pour
the cooking liquid into a saucepan.
Boil to reduce, add the strained fish
stock and boil to reduce by half.
Add the cream and boil for 1–2
minutes. Remove from the heat
and whisk in the remaining butter,
cut into dice. Stir in the remaining
herbs and serve with the sea bass.

BRAISED TURBOT WITH SORREL

1 SMALL TURBOT, ABOUT 900 G/
   2 LB, GUTTED, GILLS AND FINS
   REMOVED
2 BUNCHES OF SORREL, ABOUT
   85 G/3 OZ IN TOTAL
SALT AND PEPPER
2 SHALLOTS, FINELY CHOPPED
85 ML/3 FL OZ DRY WHITE WINE
85 ML/3 FL OZ DOUBLE CREAM
25 G/1 OZ BUTTER, CUT INTO
   SMALL CUBES

SERVES 2

Begin by soaking the fish in ice-cold water for 5–6 hours.

Preheat the oven to 200°C/400°F/Gas Mark 6. Dry the fish thoroughly.

Pull the tender parts of the sorrel leaves away from the tough central ribs. Wash the leaves and pat dry, then roll up each leaf tightly like a cigar and cut into very fine ribbons (a chiffonade).

Season the turbot on both sides. Butter a baking dish and sprinkle with the chopped shallots. Place the fish on top, dark skin upwards, and pour in the wine. Cook in the preheated oven for 20–25 minutes.

When the fish is cooked, transfer to a dish to keep hot. Pour the cooking liquid and shallots into a saucepan over high heat. Boil until the liquid is syrupy and reduced to 2–3 tablespoons. Add the cream and bring briefly to the boil, then stir in the chiffonade of sorrel. Bring back to the boil and season to taste. Remove from the heat and beat in the butter, little by little. Keep the sauce warm.

Peel off the dark skin from the fish and remove the fringe of bones by running a sharp knife around the edge of the fish and pushing the bones outwards. Place it on a hot, lightly buttered serving dish and pour over some of the sorrel sauce. Serve the remaining sauce separately.

JOHN DORY
with spring vegetables

1 JOHN DORY, ABOUT 900 G/2 LB,
   FILLETED AND SKINNED, OR
   FILLETS OF SOLE, MONKFISH,
   TURBOT OR BASS
1 POTATO, DICED
20 TINY GREEN BEANS
1 CARROT, JULIENNED (PAGE 29)
1 LEEK, WHITE PART ONLY,
   JULIENNED
1 CELERY STALK, FROM THE INSIDE
   OF THE HEAD OF CELERY,
   JULIENNED
25 G/1 OZ BUTTER
6 TABLESPOONS DOUBLE CREAM
SALT AND PEPPER
1 BUNCH OF CHIVES, FINELY
   CHOPPED

SERVES 2

Cut the fish fillets into strips about
1 cm/½ inch wide.

Cook the potato in lightly
salted boiling water until tender.
Cook the beans in lightly salted
boiling water until just tender;
drain and refresh in cold water. Put
the julienne vegetable strips in a
small saucepan with a pinch of salt,
3 tablespoons water and 1 teaspoon
of the butter. Cook over high heat
until the carrots are just tender and
the liquid has almost evaporated.
Keep all the vegetables hot.

Put the cream in a saucepan,
add a little salt and the strips of
fish. Bring to the boil and simmer
for 2 minutes – not a second more.
Place a strainer over a liquidizer
and pour in the cream. Return the
fish to the saucepan and add the
drained beans and julienne
vegetables. Add half the cooked
potato to the liquidizer and purée
until smooth. Add the remaining
butter and blend briefly. Season to
taste. Pour over the fish and
vegetables and bring to the boil
over high heat. Stir in the chives
and serve at once.

GARLIC CHICKEN CASSEROLE

1 CHICKEN, ABOUT 1.8 KG/4 LB,
   CUT INTO 4 PIECES
SALT AND PEPPER
4 TABLESPOONS EXTRA VIRGIN
   OLIVE OIL
100 G/3½ OZ SHALLOTS, CHOPPED
1 SPRIG OF ROSEMARY
3 SAGE LEAVES
200 G/7 OZ GARLIC, PEELED
200 G/7 OZ TOMATOES, SKINNED
   (PAGE 28), SEEDED AND DICED
85 G/3 OZ PITTED BLACK OLIVES
1 TABLESPOON CHOPPED FRESH
   PARSLEY

SERVES 4

Season the chicken pieces. Heat half the oil in a large casserole, add the chicken and brown on all sides. Add the shallots, rosemary and sage, cover the casserole and cook over low heat for 40–50 minutes, until the chicken is cooked.

Meanwhile, place the garlic in a saucepan with 1 litre/1¾ pints water and bring to the boil. Discard the water, replace with fresh water and bring to the boil again. Repeat five times. The garlic should be meltingly tender; if not, leave it to simmer for a few minutes. Drain well.

Remove the chicken from the casserole and keep warm. Add the tomatoes to the casserole and simmer for 5 minutes. Tip the contents of the casserole into a liquidizer, blend briefly, then rub through a fine sieve.

Return the sauce to the liquidizer and add the garlic and olives. Season to taste and slowly blend in the remaining olive oil.

Return the chicken to the casserole and pour over the sauce. Reheat gently, without boiling. Serve hot, sprinkled with parsley.

MEDALLIONS OF VEAL
with lemon

1 RIPE JUICY LEMON

1 TEASPOON SUGAR

600 G/1¼ LB VEAL FILLET, CUT
    INTO PIECES AND TRIMMED OF
    FAT AND SINEWS, OR 4 VEAL
    CUTLETS, TRIMMED OF FAT

SALT AND PEPPER

125 G/4 OZ BUTTER

8 TABLESPOONS DRY WHITE WINE

2 TABLESPOONS CHOPPED FRESH
    PARSLEY

SERVES 4

Pare off the lemon zest as thinly as possible and cut into very thin strips. Place the strips in a small saucepan with a little cold water and bring to the boil. Drain and refresh in cold water. Return to the pan with the sugar and 2 tablespoons water and cook until the water has evaporated and the zest has become a beautiful bright yellow. Set aside. Cut off the lemon peel and all the pith, and cut out the lemon segments. Set aside.

Season the veal on both sides. Heat one-third of the butter in a frying pan over moderate heat; when it begins to sizzle, add the veal and cook for about 5 minutes on each side. Remove from the pan and keep warm.

Pour off the cooking butter, then deglaze (page 30) the pan with the wine, scraping up the caramelized residue from the bottom of the pan. Keeping the pan over a moderate heat, let the wine reduce to 2 tablespoons of syrupy sauce. Cut the remaining butter into small cubes and beat into the sauce. Add the parsley and season to taste.

Serve the veal on warmed plates. Add any meat juices to the sauce and pour over the veal. Garnish with the lemon segments and strips of zest and serve with a selection of vegetables.

ROAST FILLETS OF LAMB
with a gâteau of ratatouille

2½ tablespoons butter
2 tablespoons olive oil
1 small onion, diced
2 courgettes, diced
1 aubergine, diced
1 red pepper, diced
1 green pepper, diced
2 tomatoes, skinned (page 28),
    seeded and diced
1 tablespoon chopped fresh
    thyme
salt and pepper
2 eggs
1 garlic clove, chopped
6 fresh basil leaves, chopped
1–2 tablespoons crème fraîche
    (optional)
1 saddle of lamb, 1.5–1.8 kg/
    3–4 lb, boned, bones reserved

SERVES 4

Preheat the oven to 180°C/350°F/
Gas Mark 4. Use 1 tablespoon of
the butter to grease four round
moulds, about 10 cm/4 inches
in diameter.

Heat the oil in a frying pan and
sauté the vegetables until just
tender, adding the thyme, salt and
pepper. Beat the eggs in a large
bowl and mix in the vegetables,
garlic and basil, and the cream, if
using. Spoon into the buttered
moulds and cook in the preheated
oven for about 20 minutes or until
just set. Remove from the oven
and keep warm.

Increase the oven temperature
to 240°C/475°F/Gas Mark 9.

Brown the bones, with a little
olive oil, in a roasting pan over
high heat. Add ½ tablespoon butter
and the lamb fillets and brown well
all over. Roast in the hot oven for
10 minutes; they should still be
pink in the centre. Keep the lamb
warm while you make the sauce.

Pour off the fat and add 200 ml/
7 fl oz water to the bones in the
roasting pan. Place over medium-
high heat and boil to reduce by
half. Strain into a small jug. Heat
the remaining 1 tablespoon butter
in a small saucepan until it foams
and turns light brown, then add to
the sauce.

Unmould the vegetable cakes
on to warmed serving plates. Slice
the lamb thinly and arrange around
the vegetables, with a little sauce
poured over. Serve immediately.

STUFFED SADDLE OF RABBIT

2 YOUNG RABBITS, ABOUT 1.5 KG/
  3 LB EACH
4 TABLESPOONS OLIVE OIL
4 SHALLOTS, CHOPPED
400 ML/14 FL OZ DRY WHITE WINE
1 SPRIG OF THYME
2 BAY LEAVES
1 GARLIC CLOVE
200 G/7 OZ BUTTER
2 LEEKS, WHITE PART ONLY,
  JULIENNED (PAGE 29)
2 CARROTS, JULIENNED
2 COURGETTES, JULIENNED
1 SMALL STICK OF CELERY,
  JULIENNED
½ BUNCH OF PARSLEY, FINELY
  CHOPPED
10 BASIL LEAVES, FINELY CHOPPED
2 EGG YOLKS
SALT AND PEPPER

SERVES 6–8

Prepare the saddles of rabbit (page 30) and set aside. Chop the bones and front legs and brown in a large saucepan with half the oil. When well browned, pour off the fat, add the shallots and cook for about 5 minutes or until softened. Deglaze (page 30) with half of the wine and boil to reduce by half. Add the thyme, bay leaves, garlic and water to cover; simmer gently for 1 hour.

Melt 25 g/1 oz of the butter in a saucepan and cook the vegetables until just tender. Stir in the parsley, basil, egg yolks, salt and pepper.

Place the boned saddles on a board, season and spread each with about 4 tablespoons of the vegetable mixture. Tie to form neat shapes. Preheat the oven to 220°C/425°F/Gas Mark 7.

Strain the stock through a sieve, pressing on the bones to extract all the liquid. Strain again, through a muslin-lined sieve, then return to the cleaned saucepan and boil to reduce to 250 ml/8 fl oz.

Heat the remaining oil and 25 g/1 oz butter in a roasting pan over high heat and brown the saddles all over, then cover with foil and roast in the hot oven for 10 minutes. Keep the rabbit warm while you make the sauce.

Dice the remaining butter. Pour off the fat from the roasting pan and deglaze with the remaining wine. Add the stock, bring back to the boil, then, over low heat, whisk in the butter. Slice the rabbit and serve with the sauce.

DUCK COOKED IN WINE
with apples and prunes

1 DUCK, 2–2.5 KG/4½–5½ LB,
    CUT INTO SERVING PIECES,
    BONES RESERVED
1 SMALL STICK OF CELERY, SLICED
1 CARROT, SLICED
1 ONION, SLICED
3 GARLIC CLOVES, SLICED
1 BOUQUET GARNI (PAGE 28)
1 BOTTLE FULL-BODIED RED WINE
10 STONED PRUNES
10 WALNUT HALVES
25 G/1 OZ BUTTER
SALT AND PEPPER
2 TABLESPOONS PLAIN FLOUR
1 GOLDEN DELICIOUS APPLE

SERVES 2

Place the duck pieces in a large bowl with the vegetables, bouquet garni and wine. Cover and leave in a cool place to marinate for 10–12 hours. Soak the prunes.

Strain the duck and vegetables in a colander over a large saucepan. Add the prunes to the marinade, with the bouquet garni and walnuts. Simmer for 15 minutes.

Meanwhile, heat half the butter in a large flameproof casserole. Pat dry the duck legs and breasts and season. Brown the duck in the butter over low heat, skin side down, then turn and brown the flesh side. Remove and set aside.

Brown the reserved bones and the vegetables in the casserole. Pour off the fat, add the flour and cook, stirring, for 2–3 minutes. Return the legs and breasts to the pan and pour the marinade through a sieve over the duck. Reserve the prunes and walnuts. If necessary, add a little water to cover the duck and simmer gently for 45 minutes.

When the duck is cooked, remove and keep warm. Tilt the casserole and leave for a few minutes for the fat to rise.

Peel and cube the apple and fry in the remaining butter until golden. Drain and add to the duck.

Spoon off the fat from the casserole, then return to the heat and boil to reduce to about 150 ml/ 5 fl oz. Strain into a jug and discard the bones and vegetables.

Clean the casserole and add the duck, prunes, walnuts and apples. Pour the sauce over the duck, bring to the boil and simmer for 5–10 minutes.

THE BASICS

BOUQUET GARNI

A simple bouquet garni consists of a sprig of thyme, a bay leaf, a few parsley stalks and a piece of celery, tied together with a piece of kitchen string. It can be added to almost any casserole while it is cooking, and is easily removed before serving.

In a rich wine stew, or *civet*, such as the duck recipe on page 26, I would suggest a more aromatic bouquet garni, made up of 10 black peppercorns, 1 clove, 4 juniper berries, 1 sprig of thyme, 1 strip of orange peel, 1 bay leaf, and 4 sprigs of parsley, all tied up in a piece of muslin, allowing plenty of space for the ingredients to swell.

PEELING PEPPERS

The skins of red and yellow peppers can sometimes be tough and indigestible, but they become sweet and tender after grilling until they blacken. I do this with a blowtorch, but you can also grill them over a barbecue or under a very hot grill. When the skin is black and charred all over, seal them in a polythene bag until cool enough to handle. It will then be easy to peel off the skins.

SKINNING TOMATOES

In most recipes in which tomatoes are cooked, it is preferable to skin them first. Cut a cross in the top and plunge the tomato into boiling water for a few seconds, then plunge into cold water; the skins will now slip off easily.

If required, squeeze out the seeds and cut the flesh into even dice.

PREPARING ARTICHOKES

Artichokes discolour readily: to prevent this, rub them frequently with a halved lemon while you are preparing them, and have ready a bowl of cold water into which you have squeezed the other half of the lemon, adding the squeezed lemon half to the water.

Snap off the stalks and slice off the top 4 cm/1½ inches of leaves, using a serrated knife. Pull off the outer layers of leaves, then trim the base and stalk with a sharp knife. As you prepare the artichokes, drop them into the bowl of lemon water.

For artichoke hearts, take the artichokes out of the water one at a time and trim off the inner leaves. Remove the hairy choke with a teaspoon and replace in the lemon water until all the artichokes are ready to cook.

JULIENNE STRIPS

Vegetables such as carrots, celery, courgettes and leeks are often cut into lengths known as julienne strips; this helps them to cook quickly and evenly and makes an attractive presentation. The size of these strips varies from as small as a matchstick to about 5 cm/2 inches long and 5 mm/¼ inch thick.

To cut regular julienne strips, first trim or top and tail the vegetable, then cut into the lengths you need. Slice downwards to the required thickness, then turn the slices on to their sides and cut into strips.

DEGLAZING

Simple, quick and flavoursome sauces are made by the deglazing method. After the meat or fish has been cooked it is removed from the pan, excess fat poured off, and wine, stock or water added to the pan. The pan is then placed over heat and stirred to loosen the residue and absorb the flavours back into the liquid.

The sauce can then be strained to make it smooth, or boiled to concentrate the flavours, or thickened by whisking in cubes of cold butter.

TESTING FISH

For round fish, e.g. sea bass, push a thin skewer into the centre of the fish. Leave for a few seconds, then bring the skewer close to your lower lip. If it is hot the fish is cooked; if it is cold, cook the fish for a few more minutes.

For flat fish, e.g. turbot, press your index finger down firmly on the backbone, just below the head. If you can feel the bone, the fish is cooked.

PREPARING SADDLE OF RABBIT

Cut the legs off the rabbit above the thighs and at the shoulders to keep only the main part of the back, the saddle. (The thighs can be used in another dish, and the rest of the bones should be reserved to make a stock for the sauce.)

Bone the saddle from the inside, running a small sharp knife around the bones to free them from the flesh and removing them carefully.

THE MASTER CHEFS

SOUPS
ARABELLA BOXER

THE MAIN COURSE
ROGER VERGÉ

MEZE, TAPAS AND ANTIPASTI
AGLAIA KREMEZI

ROASTS
JANEEN SARLIN

PASTA SAUCES
GORDON RAMSAY

WILD FOOD
ROWLEY LEIGH

RISOTTO
MICHELE SCICOLONE

PACIFIC
JILL DUPLEIX

SALADS
CLARE CONNERY

CURRIES
PAT CHAPMAN

MEDITERRANEAN
ANTONY WORRALL THOMPSON

HOT AND SPICY
PAUL AND JEANNE RANKIN

VEGETABLES
PAUL GAYLER

THAI
JACKI PASSMORE

LUNCHES
ALASTAIR LITTLE

CHINESE
YAN-KIT SO

COOKING FOR TWO
RICHARD OLNEY

VEGETARIAN
KAREN LEE

FISH
RICK STEIN

DESSERTS
MICHEL ROUX

CHICKEN
BRUNO LOUBET

CAKES
CAROLE WALTER

SUPPERS
VALENTINA HARRIS

COOKIES
ELINOR KLIVANS

THE MASTER CHEFS

This edition produced for The Book People Ltd,
Hall Wood Avenue, Haydock, St Helens WA11 9UL

Text © copyright 1996 Roger Vergé

Roger Vergé has asserted his right to be
identified as the Author of this Work.

Photographs © copyright 1996 Simon Wheeler

First published in 1996 by
WEIDENFELD & NICOLSON
THE ORION PUBLISHING GROUP
ORION HOUSE
5 UPPER ST MARTIN'S LANE
LONDON WC2H 9EA

All rights reserved. No part of this publication may be
reproduced, stored in a retrieval system, or
transmitted in any form or by any means, electronic,
mechanical or otherwise, without prior permission of
the copyright holder.

British Library Cataloguing-in-Publication data
A catalogue record for this book is available
from the British Library.

ISBN 0 297 83638 2

DESIGNED BY THE SENATE
EDITOR MAGGIE RAMSAY
FOOD STYLIST JOY DAVIES
ASSISTANT KATY HOLDER